.. ..   Class ....

Author ....

Title ....

ISBN: 0-9554015-0-X
       978-0-9554015-0-3

Published in 2006 by Inner City Tales
First Edition

Designed by: John Roe
Printed by: Philtone Litho Limited, Fishponds, Bristol
www.innercitytales.com

Inner city
tales

Tales
of when
society fails

By Lawrence Hoo

Innocence

One of the most important parts of a child's development is information.

It is important for children to receive the correct information to fulfill, inspire, guide and educate them so they can achieve their potential.

Children are innocent, trusting and vulnerable. We must do all we can to protect them.

Children are our future.

Dedicated to my sons

Myles, Caed and Soul for giving me the strength to see this through.

I love you

Think

All I have is a pen and a book
To write down things to make people take a conscious look

A conscious look at how situations arise
By viewing them through someone else's eyes

Please take a moment to read and think
While allowing these words to sink

To sink deep into your mind
So when you see these situations you won't be so blind

Blind to how your environment can be your biggest teacher
So I hope these tales help to create a clearer picture

Contents

Foreword

Aspire to inspire and be inspired. That's my motto it has been for 25 years and it hasn't let me down yet. I want the phrase to work in Inner City Tales too which I am proud to be a part of.

Lawrence and I grew up together from the age of 5. We shared the same city, the same community, moved among the same people although our paths never crossed to my knowledge. Not even once. As teenagers we went in different directions, made different choices and consequently had different outcomes.

Years later we met for the first time in our late 30's.

Lawrence and I actually met for the first time at the launch of an event in Bristol called Different Pasts, Shared Futures. The funny thing was I bumped into a good friend of his Michael, a few weeks before who told me of Lawrence and his passion for a clean environment and youth development. Little did I know that this thought provoking, intelligent and tenacious individual would introduce himself at this event completely out of the blue!

After a brief introduction I was inspired to meet him again. At the time I was working on a Series of items for ITV West News called Life on the Street. We arranged to meet at St Paul's learning centre for a quick chat. 3 hours later we were still chatting and a news feature was born.

I was struck by Lawrence's determination to see justice in his community. I mean real justice. Coming from someone who had lived and seen life for what it was, his experience was not to be envied.

His troubled upbringing has much to bear. For example his battle with family life as a child, and going into care. His feeling of displacement and coping with rejection. Not to mention his unenviable life on the street. Lawrence described himself as a product of his environment and confessed in his own words he was a 'nightmare'.

I paint a generic picture of an unsettled childhood, but things took a dramatic change for the worst when Lawrence was diagnosed with cancer. His challenge now was to live. By now he was in his 20's and with the fear of his life ebbing away his resolve went from bad to worse and drug abuse took hold. Bring on a whole new life existence.
I was compelled to hear his story and he told me much more than I feel able to share.

By now a televisual story was unfolding in my mind. I thought for a long time of how I would tell his story in 3 minutes and which bits I should edit, because it was all tellable. Really a documentary was the answer.

Not that he's opinionated, more passionate. Of the many issues expressed, he spoke of a hostel housing paedophiles close to where children go to school and live, of a drugs den which after a struggle with various authority figures managed to get closed down. He spoke of prostitution and drug dealing in full view of young children and their parents, and how all this was allowed to happen. And why

His whole emphasis was based on child protection; drawing from his own experience he's qualified to PhD level in why children should grow up as children and not corrupted little people.

Lawrence's poetry captures the mood perfectly. Its clear, precise and cutting. When you read this book you will get the point. Lawrence cannot sit back and allow environmental cancer to claim our children.

He cannot relax knowing that prostitution and drug dealing operate hand in hand outside the school gates. He cannot sit on the fence knowing that his children, yours and mine are exposed to social decay at best and destruction and death at worst.

And his searching enquiring eyes ask the questions, 'Why is this allowed to happen? Who is in control? Who is in charge? And who is to blame?'

Lawrence has penetrated the system and is making waves, making connections and has already begun to make changes. The change comes from within first of course and that is the catalyst of reform here I think.

The ultimate aim is for this change to have the desired effect on our children of today and tomorrow. This change should bring about true caring authorities, resulting in positive responsive communities, flourishing schools and teachers and as a result bright, motivated, confident and able children. Wouldn't that be great?

In summing up, I would like to draw from Lawrence's own words that were transmitted at the end of my news piece. He said 'A lot of people sometimes look at the kids from certain inner city communities and wonder why they frown, why they are quite angry. Well if they witnessed what the children witnessed on a daily basis, then they might find it hard to smile.'

Read this book and be inspired to inspire and join with Lawrence in making a difference in our community for the benefit of our communities and our children.

Sherrie Eugene
Broadcaster

Life

To all the people shopping at the mall
Going to purchase something big or small

Do you really know about our life?
Living where drugs and vice are rife

Let me open your eyes to the life we live
Don't worry I'm not going to ask you to give

Just listen

As I walk the streets with my eyes wide open
These are the things I see that need to be spoken

Crack heads, smack heads and ho's loitering on the street
Perverts, punters and police circling the beat

Round and round their lives continually spinning
Can you tell me out of this game who is winning?

Who really cares about all this pain?
Who is really responsible and what do they gain?

If you listen to the news they make it all sound so plain
It's the yardies that bring the drugs over sea by plane

Have you ever thought they didn't bring this disease?
Maybe it's the authorities that brought our community to its knees

But

Could you imagine if we all had the same opportunity in life?
We might all end up happily married with 3 kids and a wife

See these are the things that surround our children day by day
When they go to schools, shops or just out to play

The children have to learn how to survive while all around is evil
How can the authorities say they treat us all as equal?

Crack Head:	Crack cocaine addict
Smack Head:	Heroin addict
Ho:	Prostitute
Punter:	A person who pays for sex with prostitutes
Yardy:	Jamaican Drug Dealer
Authorities:	Bristol City Council Avon and Somerset Police
Community:	St Paul's, Bristol Easton, Bristol

Millpond Primary School, Easton, Bristol, has approximately 195 pupils aged 3-11 in attendance.

Approximately 28 of these children aged 3-4 are in the Nursery.

Nursery Trip

I woke up again wondering if it was all going to be the same
Then I drove my son to nursery through the pouring rain

On the way we pass his brother's school where I see
Two drug addicted prostitutes looking back at me

When we pull up to his nursery gates
There are dealers and junkies engaging in their daily dates

I wonder and think how this can be for real
What must the parents and children feel?

Prostitute being supplied drugs outside Millpond Primary School, Easton, Bristol.

The sign directly above their heads reads Millpond Primary School while the one to the right reads Police Warning Kerb crawlers will be arrested and has been in place since 2002.

School Fence

How can it be right, how can it make sense
For prostitutes to be outside the school fence

Instead of removing prostitutes from the street
They put up warning signs for them to meet

To meet their punters who pull up daily
While they're standing on the corner plainly

Plainly in view for the children to see
While in school or the nursery

Why don't the school call the police?
You'd think if they did it would surely cease

But they are there day after day
Question I ask is how is it this way?

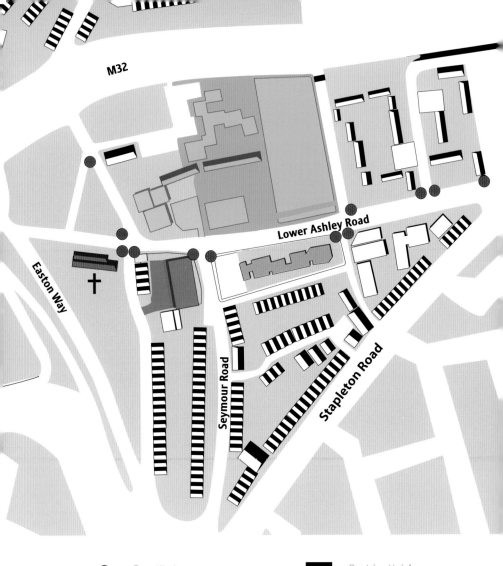

M32

Lower Ashley Road

Easton Way

Seymour Road

Stapleton Road

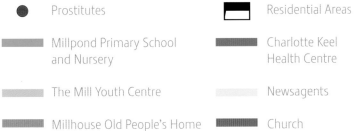

●	Prostitutes	▬	Residential Areas
	Millpond Primary School and Nursery		Charlotte Keel Health Centre
	The Mill Youth Centre		Newsagents
	Millhouse Old People's Home		Church

Shame

Look officer at what our children are going through can you imagine the pain
Oh yes I can it really is a shame

A shame, look officer these children go to school surrounded by women on the game
Oh come on now you're preaching or is it me you're trying to blame

No I know it's not your fault you're just following orders
Not to protect the children from within these borders

Well we have our priorities and robbery and theft come before your school
But isn't the theft of a child's innocence the crime most cruel?

Now look stop playing with my words we're doing our best
Oh come on now officer, give it a rest

Answer me this where do you live, do you live near?
Oh no, I live in Portishead and let me make one thing clear

We don't have many police patrolling the beat
Do you have prostitutes soliciting where your children meet?

No
Oh!!!!

Adapted from a conversation held between the author and police on Lower Ashley Road, Easton, Bristol.

Prostitute soliciting under school sign outside of Millpond Primary School, Easton, Bristol, as children walk home from school.

No More

As our children walk along the street
They have to pass prostitutes waiting for punters to meet

How much more of this must our children take?
How much more before our children break?

How much more must they endure?
How long before we say

No more?

Punter: A person who pays for sex with prostitutes

Consequences

As we watch the children grow
They start observing and thinking they know

But what does a child know about consequence from its action?
To some it will look exciting but we know it's a deadly distraction

A child could look at a dealer and just see money and wealth
But following this path could destroy their health

What about the dealer what could they say
When a naive unsuspecting child comes their way

'Yeah the life's great you make plenty money'
Truth is they've been there for years and it isn't even funny

The child gets distracted from learning while in school
All he can think about is the dealer who he sees as cool

He stops going to school, he's out on the street
Selling some 10 bags helping the dealer to eat

But before too long the child is caught
He doesn't identify the dealer, that's what he's been taught

So here now is a child with his first conviction
A convicted drug dealer logged in the system

He's gone from a child to being labelled a criminal
Can you see a pattern? It's quite subliminal

Girl On The Corner

Girl on the corner shotting on a beautiful summer's day
Cussing a female junkie who only has eight pound to pay

Junkie looks up says 'this deal ain't fair'
Girl replies 'wha you think I care'?

'You didn't have enough money to pay for your shit
Be grateful for what you've got it'll give you one good hit'

The woman stops, turns and walks away
She has enough to help her lose another day

Shotting: Dealing

Junkie: Drug addict

Prostitute soliciting 25 metres from May Park Primary School, Eastville, Bristol.

May Park Primary School, Eastville, Bristol has approximately 369 pupils aged 3 to 11 in attendance plus approximately 20 full time and 19 part time nursery places.

Another day Around The Way

I see a young girl working her beat
I look and wonder what caused her to end up on the street

You can see the beauty that has been stolen from this young life
As she's waiting for some punter cheating on his wife

A punter pulls up, she jumps in
They agree a fee, she starts sucking

In a short while the deal is done
She's been paid and he's cum

She jumps out, he drives away
She now goes to find a dealer to pay

She hands over her money in exchange for some smack
As soon as she's injected it she's straight back

Straight back working her beat
Waiting for another punter to meet

Smack: Heroin

Junkie loitering 25 metres from St. Paul's Day Nursery, St. Paul's, Bristol.

St Paul's Day Nursery, St Paul's, Bristol has approximately 40 children aged 2 - 5 attending on a part time basis.

Junkie

Junkie stood around with nowhere to go
Loitering on the corner hoping for a dealer to show

He smokes a cigarette then stubs it out
Has a look around but still no one's about

He goes to the phone box and makes a call
Then comes out and sits on the wall

Then from around the corner a car pulls up
Junkie walks over looks like he's in luck

The passenger door opens and he jumps in
An exchange is done and he leaves with a grin

Junkie: Drug addict

Needle filled with blood which has been left in the Kango building.

The Kango building is located 25 metres from St. Paul's Day Nursery, St Paul's, Bristol.

Kango

Around the corner from the nursery is a building called Kango
It's a place that a lot of junkies can go

They use it like a community centre
Knowing that people from the community are afraid to enter

The building is riddled with disease
Yet by walking through the gate you can enter with ease

They meet up there when they have drugs to share
And throw down their needles without a care

Then they settle down to rest
While waiting for their drugs to digest

Then after a while once their high has gone
They go back out onto the streets to get money for another one

Junkie: Drug addict

Play

In the middle of the night when you're safe asleep
These are the scenes on the street that would make you weep

People roaming around the streets like rats
Huddled in dark corners like alley cats

One group controlled by an uncontrollable need
The other seeing an opportunity while being powered by greed

These are the scenes of a play that is open every night
It's just around the corner and you know it can't be right

For some of these children's lives don't seem real
They would rather spend their money on drugs than a meal

I wish these were the scenes of a badly scripted play
But this is the reality for many that goes on every day

Child

Can you imagine a child living on its own?
With the streets as its house a pillow made of stone

Waking each day having to survive on the street
Dodging beatings and perverts while looking for something to eat

How do you imagine all these children feel
Going so long without a decent meal?

You can look into their eyes and see hunger and pain
How is it possible for them to take the strain?

Please give some time to understand their plight
Then you might understand that things are not right

For we have created a lost generation
By not caring enough or paying attention

View of children's play area at Jumoke Day Nursery St Paul's, Bristol.

Picture taken from Brigstocke Road Approved Premises (Bail Hostel) St Paul's, Bristol.

Jumoke Day Nursery provides approximately 30 places for children aged 2-5 years old.

Brigstocke Road Approved Premises (Bail Hostel) provides approximately 28 places and houses paedophiles as well as people who have committed other offences.

Temptation

I don't know how this can be right
I don't know how the people who allow it, sleep at night

Where we live in our community
They house paedophiles next to a nursery

I know it sounds too insane to be true
Could you imagine it happening near you?

The children pass them unaware every day
On their way to school, nursery or out to play

Who is responsible, who makes the rules?
Are they insane, or are they fools?

For what is this crazy game they're playing?
One mistake and the children will be paying

How can they put temptation so close?
Directly beneath a paedophile's nose

Paedophile: A person who is sexually attracted to children

These signs are displayed outside Millpond Primary School, Easton, Bristol.

From an early age children going to Millpond Primary School as well as other children in the community will read these signs and want to know the meaning to them.

Avon and Somerset Police Inspector Andy Bennett speaking on prostitution at an Eastville Residents Action Group meeting said:

"There is no point in spreading the problem into the four corners of Bristol because we cannot control it".

Evening Post 19th April 2006

Police Inspector Andy Bennett is the sector Inspector for Trinity.

Trinity sector covers St Paul's and Easton.

Warning Signs

The authorities don't solve crimes
They put up warning signs

To warn people that come from outside
That it's a lot safer if they stay locked in their ride

Robbers beware, Police operations in this area
If you read these signs as a kid would they scare ya?

Don't flash your cash or mobile phone
You are now entering an inner city zone

Police warning, Kerb crawlers will be arrested
But the truth is they have an interest that is vested

A vested interest to confine it to one zone
So they can all feel safe when they go home

Authorities: Bristol City Council
                Avon and Somerset Police

Ride: Car

Routine Check!

Police stop and check a local business man on Ashley road,
St Paul's, Bristol.

He has committed no offence, has no criminal record and is a fully
licensed driver.

Something's not right

A wealth of knowledge can make dreams a reality
Each and every one of us has the ability

The potential inside just needs to be released
But first we have to address the way we're policed

Our environment creates many problems that we have to face daily
They leave a lasting impression on our children mainly

The police stop and search local people on a regular basis
Yet junkies and ho's hang around in open spaces

They have no problems applying their trade
But when the police pull over a local driver it's a full scale raid

For what reason are these people allowed to come into our community?
The time has come for us to show common unity

We must voice our concerns until we are heard
Because the situation has become absurd

Junkie: Drug addict

Ho: Prostitute

Community: St Paul's, Bristol
                 Easton, Bristol

Bury a friend

A group of youths are gathered, it's late at night
An argument starts and two begin to fight

Through the mayhem a girl is hurt
Some of the youths look around then they splurt

The girl's people get to hear the news
They can't believe it, they're confused

People get angry, they go and look for the few
They know who they are, they know the crew

They go in search and look around
Not stopping until they are found

Then they run up on them, asking who dun it
But one is over ready and starts to hit

Then one pulls out a knife and drives it in
The youth's in shock, stops breathing

As he drops and falls to the ground
It goes all quiet, no one makes a sound

Then some people turn around and run
And now we are back where we begun

A group of youths have gone to spread the news
Now there will be more people looking for crews

The question I ask is when will it end?
Because I don't want it to become common, to bury a friend

Splurt: Go

Another Way

There needs to be another way
The predator can become the prey

The strong can become weak, the wild can become meek
And in the end we will realise we're on a losing streak

For the avenues that are being created for people to follow
Will leave us empty of substance, completely hollow

Jail Time

I hear the authorities say they want to increase jail time
Do they believe it's the answer to inner city crime?

They say they carry weapons to look hard
Have they ever thought they're scared and on guard

Scared of the environment that they have been left in to grow
Now the consequences of other people's actions are starting to show

For in many major cites you have a place labelled a ghetto
Where the people have been neglected with no help to grow

The authorities help to keep the people held down
By allowing these places to be the drugs and vice capital of town

Everyone in the city can tell you it's the place they sell drugs
Yet people act surprised that it breeds young thugs?

Society has to take some of the blame
For allowing these children to grow around such a deadly game

Can you imagine living in their reality
Where violent crime, drugs and prostitution are the normality?

They have to grow witnessing these things every day
Things aren't so black and white when you look at them this way

The problem is much bigger than increasing jail time
From when they allowed these children to grow up surrounded by crime

Vice Centre

The authorities allowed our community to become a drug and vice centre
That they themselves became too afraid to enter

How did things become so bad in this place?
It's an absolute disgrace

For all these things to be going on
There must be something very wrong

The authorities cannot care
For so long, we haven't been treated fair

How many potentials have not been realised?
Because our community has been victimised

Authorities: Bristol City Council
               Avon and Somerset Police

Community: St Paul's, Bristol
             Easton, Bristol

Cheltenham Road

M32

Bond Street

The Haymarket

St Paul's

Development Area

Broadmead

Map shows development area's location to St. Paul's.

Development Plan

Now comes the new development plan
Now the authorities want these things to go as fast as they can

They start to move people and make the community disperse
Because in their eyes we just make things worse

I mean let me tell you about a few years ago
When there was nowhere safe for the children to go?

So many people put in to exchange
To get their children out of the firing range

But that was all part of the scam
To make people relocate was their plan

But in a few years it will be all good
By then it will no longer be our neighbourhood

Authorities: Bristol City Council
Avon and Somerset Police
Places for People (Bristol Churches Housing Association)
Knightstone Housing Association

One of many properties in St. Paul's, Bristol that local Housing Authorities sealed once tenants had been moved.

Many of the properties were in desperate need of repairs and updating due to lack of maintenance by the Housing Authorities.

Regeneration Zone

I watch the children playing by their home
But worry because they're living in a regeneration zone

Where the games they play will no longer be tolerated
Because their community has been decimated

Picked, plucked and taken apart
Like someone reaching in and ripping out your heart

For many of the people they knew while growing
Are no longer here and the change is showing

Authorities: Bristol City Council
                Places for People (Bristol Churches Housing Association)
                Knightstone Housing Association

One of nine four storey Victorian town houses on Ashley Road, St Paul's, Bristol, which have all been neglected by Places for People (Bristol Churches Housing Association) over a period of years.

Squatters Mansions

Squatters contact Knightstone housing association to make sure it's OK
Then they break into one of their properties, make it a new place to stay

They live there for free, taking drugs, making noise and getting high
But Knightstone do nothing to move them and we wonder why

The authorities use ASBOs to evict tenants who they want to relocate
But allow squatters to stay in our community and make it a state

Other tenants they offer money to leave and a new home
So that they clear us from their regeneration zone

The authorities say people's rent or council tax hasn't been paid
But this could be because the applications have been delayed

Delayed through a system that isn't able to cope
But if they're not processed quick enough they have no hope

No hope to stay in the community where they have grown
No hope of any mercy being shown

How can it be right for them to collude like this?
Stopping properties from being available to people on the housing list

Authorities: Bristol City Council
                Places for People (Bristol Churches Housing Association)
                Knightstone Housing Association

View of part of the expansion area 16/5/06 with St Paul's church, St Paul's in the background.

Expansion

Now the authorities start to use the full power of the law
To stop undesirables from coming into St. Paul's any more

Cameras are installed to monitor people as they walk along the street
Making it harder for the dealers and junkies to meet

The junkies get stopped, searched and generally given grief
To make sure that their visit is brief

They start to move on the kerb crawlers that circle our borders
Because prostitution must be moved are the new orders

They remove all people from the places that were used for dealing
Combined with the above you can see the community healing

It is so different from a few years ago
When you could be knocked down by their continuous flow

I wonder and think what could have started this, what does it mean?
Then I remember the Broadmead expansion scheme

The £500 million investment seems responsible for the change
For that reason alone our problems have come within their range

They don't want the problems we have had to deal with to become theirs
That's why the area's being cleaned up and it seems like everyone cares

But what about the years, all the years before
When no one cared for our community it was just looked down on as poor

Why were we not given the same protection?
Then it was like everyone was looking in a different direction

Authorities: Bristol City Council
                Avon and Somerset Police

Two flats and a maisonette of many properties sold in St. Paul's by the Housing Authorities since 2005.

Game over

So many have been sealed and secured
So many people homeless that need bed and board

What is the reason that these properties have laid empty
So they could say they're uninhabitable, but still sell them for plenty

But what has been the cost to the community
How can they do this, don't they feel guilty?

They used these properties to bring the community down
Now they have moved people to different parts of town

The investors come around and have a look
Dividing up the community with the auction book

And soon the properties will be sold to their new owners
That will mean that phase one is over

Housing Authorities: Bristol City Council
                         Places for People (Bristol Churches Housing)
                         Knightstone Housing Association

Sign shows roundabout at junction 3 of the M 32.

M 32

The authorities say the situation has improved
Really the problem has just been moved

Moved across the M 32 to a new destination
Making Easton the new ghetto in creation

For all the problems that used to be here
Will soon have Easton gripped in fear

Who makes the decisions that are playing with our lives?
They say they're trying to help but the truth is they're full of lies

From they allow prostitutes to work outside of our schools
They can't care for our children they're treating us like fools

Authorities: Bristol City Council
                Avon and Somerset Police

ASBOs bypass the ordinary Crown Court system by allowing police and local authorities to apply to magistrates for orders restricting the movement of individuals. Applications are rarely refused.

Mr. Blair's Respect Bill will also deprive anti-social families of their own homes.

A senior official told The Mail on Sunday: "The problem we have is that while local authorities can apply considerable pressure on those living in council accommodation, there is little we can do currently about owner-occupiers".

A spokeswoman for Liberty said: "Respect needs to be a two-way street. Creating a ghetto where you put an entire family because of the crimes of one individual is wrong".

Mail on Sunday 9th October 2005

Control Zones

The authorities want to create control zones
Where they will ban people from leaving their homes

First they introduce the ASBO
Then over time its power will grow

To allow them to evict people only to re-house them somewhere new
A place where they belong in their point of view

A place not near and out of sight
But not too far so they can pop in at night

They will use the law to ban people from entering other zones
Effectively imprisoning people in their homes

Hostage

Until we stop allowing ourselves to be abused, we're a hostage
Until we make a stand for our rights, we're a hostage

We're the hostage, society is our captor
Now has come the time to write a new chapter

Don't stand by as if nothing can change
It's within our power to make it re-arrange

Self

When life doesn't feel worth living
And no one around is forgiving

This is the time to

Look into yourself

Believe in yourself

Fight for yourself

Be true to yourself

Because maybe one day all that you will have is

Yourself

Truth

In life it can be hard to know what to do
Always try to be true to yourself and you will shine through

It might not happen immediately, it could take a while
But in the end you will be able to smile

By understanding and knowing that your intentions are right
And actually knowing that you can win the fight

The fight to be all you can
Whether you're a boy, girl, woman, or man

Unite

So many things are not right
What we need to do is unite

We have to come together to win this fight
Combining all our powers, strength and might

What can we do in a small group?
See that was their greatest coup

Separating, segregating and dividing us all
Then telling us that our problems are small

Don't you see that many of our problems are common?
We need to stop looking at each other as foreign

For we are all one family
Don't let them create our destiny

The time has come for us to rise
Question them and expose their lies

Destiny

The journey is long and much strength is needed
To reverse the cycle that has preceded

But that is no surprise, who ever thought it would be easy
To restore self belief to the disposed and needy

No matter how hard the path is to travel
This is a riddle we will unravel

When we do our people will be free
And we will be able to reach our destiny

I would like to thank all who supported me and donated the money that enabled me to make this book a reality

Kuumba
Puma
Elite Solicitors
Live/Let Property Management
Full Cycle
Georgina's Hair and beauty
Afro Delight
Café Maiteya
Select Finance
Morgan's Estate Agents
Top Shop St Pauls
C&C Tyres
Tangys
Brunel Associates
Central Estate agents
M32 News/Off Licence

Helen Wilson
Andrew Samuels
Tony Kear
Madge Dresser
Wilf Summerbe
Kweku
Daga

www.innercitytales.com